FREE STUFF FOR KIDS

OUR PLEDGE

We have collected and examined the best free and up-to-a-dollar* offers that we could find. Each supplier of items in this book has promised to honor properly made requests for **single items** throughout 1991. Though mistakes do happen, we are doing our best to make sure this book really works.

*Plus a few extra-special over-a-dollar values!

Meadowbrook
Distributed by Simon & Schuster
New York

DEDICATION

To Pat Blakely, Barbara Haislet, and **Judith Hentges** for creating and publishing the original *Rainbow Book,* and for proving that children, parents, and teachers would respond enthusiastically to a source of free things by mail. They taught us the importance of carefully checking the quality of each item and doing our best to make sure that each and every child's request is satisfied.

Library of Congress Cataloging-in-Publication data

Free stuff for kids
      p. cm. Includes index
      Summary: Contains listings for over 350 things that can be ordered free of charge or for under $1.00.
      1. Free material—Juvenile literature. [1. Free material.] I. Meadowbrook Creations
AG600.F684   1990b   011'.03—dc20   89.3386

ISBN: 0-88166-141-4

The Free Stuff Editors
Director: Bruce Lansky
Editorial Coordinator: Ramona Czer
Production: David Garbe

Simon & Schuster Ordering Number: 0-671-72562-9

90 91 5 4 3 2 1

Copyright © 1976, 1977, 1979, 1980, 1981, 1982, 1983, 1984, 1985, 1986, 1987, 1988, 1989, 1990 by Meadowbrook Creations

Published by Meadowbrook Press, 18318 Minnetonka Boulevard, Deephaven, MN 55391.

BOOK TRADE DISTRIBUTION by Simon & Schuster; a division of Simon and Schuster, Inc., 1230 Avenue of the Americas, New York, NY 10020.

Printed in the United States of America

what's inside

about this book

Free Stuff for Kids contains listings of over 350 items children can send away for. We have examined every item and think they are among the best offers available. There are no trick offers—only safe, fun, and informative things kids like!

Each supplier has promised to honor properly made requests for **single items** through **1991.** This book is revised each year, with some suppliers and offers changing each time. <u>If you use this edition</u> *<u>**after 1991**</u>, <u>your request might not be honored</u>

The book is designed for independent use by children who can read and write. Directions in Chapter 1 tell exactly how to request an item. Instructions for each item are consistent. Half the fun for kids is knowing they can use the book on their own. The other half is getting a real reward for their efforts!

Our heartfelt appreciation goes to hundreds of organizations and individuals for making this book possible. The suppliers and editors of this book have a common goal: to make it possible for children to reach out and discover the world by themselves.

USING THIS BOOK

using this book

working with this book

Before sending for free stuff, get your book in shape. Fold it open one page at a time, working from the two ends toward the middle. This will make the book lie flat when you read or copy addresses.

reading carefully

Read descriptions carefully and find out exactly what you are getting. Here are some guidelines to help you know what you are sending for:

- A pamphlet or folder is usually one sheet of paper folded over and printed on both sides.
- A booklet is usually larger and contains more pages, but it is smaller than a book.

following directions

It is important to follow each supplier's directions. You might need to use a postcard. Or you might need paper and an envelope. If you do not follow the directions **exactly,** you will not get what you request. Ask for only one of anything you send for.

Note to teachers: Please do not submit requests for multiple copies. Also, *do not* keep using the same edition year after year. Each year, we update our book, taking out old items, inserting new ones, and changing addresses and prices. Obtaining the most recent edition assures you and your class that all requests will be honored.

sending postcards

A postcard is a small card you can write on and send through the mail without an envelope. Many suppliers offering **free** items require you to send requests on postcards. Please do this. It saves them the time it takes to open many envelopes.

You can buy postcards at the post office with stamps already on them. Or you can buy cards and put stamps on them. You must use a card that is at least 3½ by 5½ inches. (The post office **will not** take 3-by-5-inch index cards.)

Your postcards should look like this. Neatly print your return address and the supplier's address on the side with the stamp. Neatly print your request, your name, and your address on the other side. Do not abbreviate the name of your street or city.

Jessie Rogers
2415 Lake Street
Solon Springs, WI 54873

United States Olympic Committee
Dept. OL84
1750 E. Boulder St.
Colorado Springs, CO 80909

Dear Sir or Madam:

Please send me a copy of the Olympic Games booklet.

Thank you very much.

Sincerely yours,
Jessie Rogers
2415 Lake Street
Solon Springs, WI 54873

sending letters

Your letters should look like this. If you are including coins or a return envelope, say so in the letter.

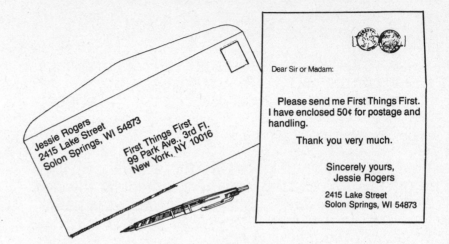

Jessie Rogers
2415 Lake Street
Solon Springs, WI 54873

First Things First
99 Park Ave., 3rd Fl.
New York, NY 10016

Dear Sir or Madam:

Please send me First Things First. I have enclosed 50¢ for postage and handling.

Thank you very much.

Sincerely yours,
Jessie Rogers

2415 Lake Street
Solon Springs, WI 54873

- Neatly print the name of the item you want **exactly** as you see it in the directions.

- Neatly print your own name and address. Do not abbreviate the name of your street or city.

- Put a first-class stamp (they cost 25¢) on any envelope you send unless instructed to do otherwise. You can get stamps at the post office.

sending money

If the directions say to enclose money for postage and handling, please tape coins to your letter so they won't break out of your envelope. Don't stack coins on top of each other. If an item costs $1.00, send a one-dollar bill instead of coins. Don't tape dollar bills. **Send only U.S. money.**

sending a long envelope

If the directions say to enclose a long, self-addressed, stamped envelope, here's how to do it. First, write your name and address on a 9½-inch-long envelope as if you were mailing it to yourself. Put a first-class stamp on it. Then fold it up and put it inside another 9½-inch-long envelope to the supplier and put a first-class stamp on it.

waiting

Expect to wait four to eight weeks for your free stuff to arrive. Sometimes you have to wait longer. Remember, suppliers get thousands of requests each year. Please be patient.

making sure you get what you send for

We've tried to make the directions for using this book as clear as possible because we want you to get what you send for. But you must follow **all** directions exactly as they're written, or the supplier will not be able to answer your request.

When asking for free stuff:

- **Do not** ask for more than **one** of an item.

- **Do** print your name, address, and zip code clearly and fully on the postcard or on the envelope **and** letter you send. **Do not** abbreviate either one! Sometimes envelopes and letters get separated after they reach the supplier.

- **Do** send the correct amount of money, but use as few coins as possible. **Do not** send pennies. Send **U.S.** money only.

- **Do** tape the coins you send to the letter you send them with. If you don't, the money might rip the envelope and fall out. **Do not** stack the coins in the envelope.

- **Do** use a 9½-inch-long, self-addressed, stamped envelope if the instructions say you should.

- **Do not** ask Meadowbrook to send you any of the items listed in the book. We don't have these supplies on hand.

Please follow the rules and avoid disappointment.

What to do if you are unsatisfied:

If you have complaints about any offer, or if you don't receive the items you sent for within 8-10 weeks, please let us know. (Before you complain, please reread the directions. Are you sure you followed them properly?) We won't be able to send you the item, but we can make sure that any suppliers who didn't fulfill requests they receive from kids are dropped from next year's edition of *Free Stuff for Kids*.

We'd also like to know which offers you like and what kind of new offers you'd like us to add to next year's edition. So don't be bashful—write us a letter. Send your complaints or suggestions to:

The Free Stuff Editors
Meadowbrook Press
18318 Minnetonka Blvd.
Deephaven, MN 55391

7
COMPLAINTS

HEY, SPORT!

10 PRO TEAMS

fan-tastic

Football fans, this offer is for you! All 28 National Football League teams listed below offer a fan-mail package loaded with great giveaways. Most include a team sticker, an 8½-by-11-inch card with photos of team stars on one side and team facts on the flip side, an official NFL schedule, a map showing the locations of all the NFL teams, plus information about the Football Hall of Fame and the NFL Superpro Club.

directions:	Use a postcard. (Free)
ask for:	Fan Mail Package
write to:	The team of your choice from those listed below.

Atlanta Falcons
Fan Package—FSK
Suwanee Road at I-85
Suwanee, GA 30174

Buffalo Bills
Fan Package—FSK
One Bills Drive
Orchard Park, NY 14127

Chicago Bears
Fan Package—FSK
Halas Hall
250 N. Washington
Lake Forest, IL 60045

Cincinnati Bengals
Fan Package—FSK
200 Riverfront Stadium
Cincinnati, OH 45202

Cleveland Browns
Fan Package—FSK
Tower B
Cleveland Stadium
Cleveland, OH 44114

Dallas Cowboys
Fan Package—FSK
Cowboys Center
One Cowboys Parkway
Irving, TX 75063

Denver Broncos
Fan Package—FSK
5700 Logan Street
Denver, CO 80216

Detroit Lions
Fan Package—FSK
Pontiac Silverdome
P.O. Box 4200
1200 Featherstone Road
Pontiac, MI 48057

Green Bay Packers
Fan Package—FSK
P.O. Box 10628
1265 Lombardi Avenue
Green Bay, WI 54307

Houston Oilers
Fan Package—FSK
6900 Fannin Street
Houston, TX 77030

Indianapolis Colts
Fan Package—FSK
P.O. Box 535000
7001 W. 56th Street
Indianapolis, IN 46253

Kansas City Chiefs
Fan Package—FSK
One Arrowhead Drive
Kansas City, MO 64129

11
PRO TEAMS

**12
PRO TEAMS**

Los Angeles Raiders
Fan Package—FSK
332 Center Street
El Segundo, CA 90245

Los Angeles Rams
Fan Package—FSK
2327 W. Lincoln Avenue
Anaheim, CA 92801

Miami Dolphins
Fan Package—FSK
Joe Robbie Stadium
2269 NW 199th Street
Miami, FL 33056

Minnesota Vikings
Fan Package—FSK
9520 Viking Drive
Eden Prairie, MN 55344

New England Patriots
Fan Package—FSK
Sullivan Stadium, Route 1
Foxboro, MA 02035

New Orleans Saints
Fan Package—FSK
1500 Poydras Street
New Orleans, LA 70112

New York Giants
Fan Package—FSK
Giants Stadium
East Rutherford, NY 07073

New York Jets
Fan Package—FSK
598 Madison Avenue
New York, NY 10022

Philadelphia Eagles
Fan Package—FSK
Veterans Stadium
Broad Street and Pattison
   Avenue
Philadelphia, PA 19148

Phoenix Cardinals
Fan Package—FSK
51 W. Third Street
Tempe, AZ 85281

Pittsburgh Steelers
Fan Package—FSK
Three Rivers Stadium
300 Stadium Circle
Pittsburgh, PA 15212

San Diego Chargers
Fan Package—FSK
San Diego Jack Murphy
   Stadium
P.O. Box 20666
9449 Friars Road
San Diego, CA 92120

San Francisco 49ers
Fan Package—FSK
4949 Centennial Blvd
Santa Clara, CA 95054

Seattle Seahawks
Fan Package—FSK
11220 NE 53rd Street
Kirkland, WA 98033

Tampa Bay Buccaneers
Fan Package—FSK
One Buccaneer Place
Tampa, FL 33607

Washington Redskins
Fan Package—FSK
13832 Redskin Drive
Herndon, VA 22070

13
PRO TEAMS

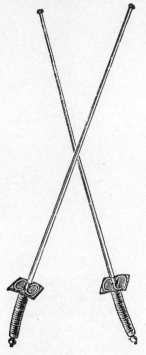

fencing decal

Get this colorful vinyl decal of the U.S. Fencing Association and show that you support young fencers who hope to enter the Olympics one day.

directions: Use paper and an envelope. You must enclose a long, self-addressed, stamped envelope **and** 50¢ for one decal.

ask for: Fencing Decal

write to: U.S.F.A.
Promotional Department
1750 E. Boulder Street
Colorado Springs, CO 80909

foiled again!

Fencing—the art of sword fighting—has been practiced for centuries, first in training for the deadly combat of the duel, and now as an Olympic sport. Send for this brochure and learn how to be a good spectator.

directions: Use paper and an envelope. You must enclose a long, self-addressed, stamped envelope.

ask for: Spectator's Brochure

write to: U.S.F.A.
Promotional Department
1750 E. Boulder Street
Colorado Springs, CO 80909

the biathlon

The biathlon is a winter Olympic sport that combines cross-country skiing and target shooting. It comes from the Scandinavian countries, but the United States also has a biathlon team. You can show your support for them by displaying this decal.

directions: Use paper and an envelope. You must enclose $1.00.

ask for: U.S. Biathlon Team Decal

write to: U.S. Biathlon Association
Free Stuff For Kids
P.O. Box 5515
Essex Junction, VT 05452

good as gold

U.S. Swimming competition isn't just about going for gold. It's about building a tradition that's as good as gold. Get two buttons to show your support.

directions: Use paper and an envelope. You must enclose a long, self-addressed, stamped envelope **and** 50¢ for **both** buttons.

ask for: Good as Gold **and** Swim-a-thon Buttons

write to: Promotions Department
United States Swimming, Inc.
1750 E. Boulder Street
Colorado Springs, CO 80909-5770

SAFE
SWIMMING
IS FUN
SWIMMING!

in the swim

Swimming is more fun when you're swimming safely. Send for this button that features Pelican Pete and his message, "Safe swimming is fun swimming."

directions: Use paper and an envelope. You must enclose 50¢ **and** a long, self-addressed, stamped envelope.

ask for: Pelican Pete Button

write to: Promotions Department
United States Swimming, Inc.
1750 E. Boulder Street
Colorado Springs, CO 80909-5770

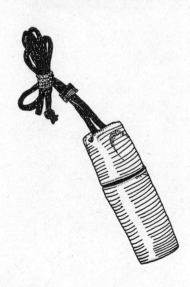

high and dry

Swimming, boating, and other water sports are a lot of fun, and this watertight, plastic cylinder is great for keeping your valuables dry at the beach, in the boat, or at the pool (1½ by 4 inches).

directions: Use paper and an envelope. You must enclose $1.00.

ask for: Swim Safe Carrier

write to: Premiums, Promotions, Purchases, Ltd.
P.O. Box 460
W. Babylon, NY 11702

tennis anyone?

Whether you're a tennis star or just starting out, you
need to know the rules of the game. This illustrated
booklet from the nonprofit U.S. Tennis Association
summarizes tennis rules from service to set.

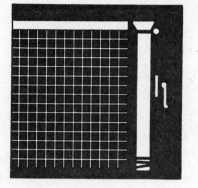

directions: Use paper and an envelope. You
must enclose $1.00.

ask for: Illustrated Introduction to the
Rules of Tennis

write to: USTA Publications
707 Alexander Road
Princeton, NJ 08540

court manners

Being a good sport is part of the game, and it makes
the game of tennis more fun for everyone. This
laminated card gives the tennis players' code of
conduct. Carry it with you to the court.

directions: Use paper and an envelope. You
must enclose 25¢.

ask for: Code of Conduct Card

write to: USTA Publications
707 Alexander Road
Princeton, NJ 08540

writing racquet

You don't usually make a *racket* when you write, but then you probably never wrote with a *racquet* before. Get this ballpoint pen that's shaped like a tennis racquet and try it for yourself.

directions: Use paper and an envelope. You must enclose $1.00.

ask for: USTA Tennis Racquet Pen

write to: USTA Publications
707 Alexander Road
Princeton, NJ 08540

it's news to you

Baseball Card News is a biweekly newspaper for people who collect baseball cards. It contains the latest news, photos, and features. Send for your free sample copy.

directions: Use a postcard. (Free)

ask for: Baseball Card News Sample Copy

write to: Baseball Card News
Department BLW
700 E. State Street
Iola, WI 54990

batter up

What can you do with a baseball bat besides swing it? You can write with it! Get this pen that's shaped like a small baseball bat. It's even autographed!

directions: Use paper and an envelope. You must enclose $1.00.

ask for: Louisville Slugger Bat Pen

write to: H & B Promotions
P.O. Box 10
Department 90 SRC
Jeffersonville, IN 47130

slug it!

What else can you do with a bat? You can have a major league key chain!

directions: Use paper and an envelope. You must enclose 90¢.

ask for: Louisville Slugger Bat Key Chain

write to: H & B Promotions
P.O. Box 10
Department 90 SRC
Jeffersonville, IN 47130

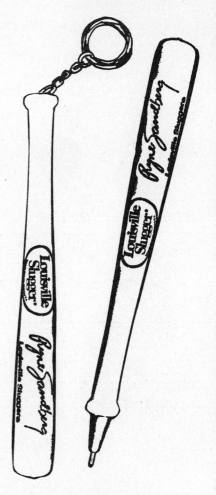

bowling tips

Do you know how to throw a strike or convert a spare? This folder shows you how to do that and more!

directions: Use paper and an envelope. You must enclose a long, self-addressed, stamped envelope.

ask for: Bif's Fun-Damentals of Bowling

write to: Young American Bowling Alliance
5301 S. 76th Street
Greendale, WI 53192

waterskiing fun

What could be better on a hot summer day than gliding through wind and water on a pair of skis! Learn about waterskiing from this pamphlet.

directions: Use paper and an envelope. You must enclose a long, self-addressed, stamped envelope.

ask for: Guide to Safe Waterskiing

write to: American Water Ski Association
799 Overlook Drive
Winter Haven, FL 33884

lost and found

Learn about orienteering, a sport where you trek through the wild using only a map and compass to find your way. You get a 10-page booklet, a sample orienteering map, and a list of orienteering clubs.

directions: Use paper and an envelope. You must enclose a long, self-addressed, stamped envelope.

ask for: Orienteering Map and Booklet

write to: Orienteering Services, USA
Department FS
P.O. Box 1604
Binghamtom, NY 13902

yo-yo trickery

Beginners can get to know their yo-yos by reading this free foldout. It even shows some yo-yo tricks.

directions: Use paper and an envelope. You must enclose a long, self-addressed, stamped envelope.

ask for: Duncan Yo-Yo Trick Sheet

write to: Duncan Toys Company
Department FSFK
P.O Box 5
Middlefield, OH 44062

start your engine

On your mark, get set, go! Get the 1990-1991 Official All-American Soap Box Derby Rule Book and learn how to enter contests and win soap box derbies.

directions: Use a postcard. (Free)

ask for: The Official All-American Soap Box Derby Rule Book

write to: All-American Soap Box Derby
P.O. Box 7233 Derby Downs
Akron, OH 44306

fishing fun

The "Fishing Fun for Kids" coloring and dot-to-dot activity book tells you how to get started fishing. Learn what to do when you feel a nibble on the line, so you'll go home with a fish and not a story.

directions: Use paper and an envelope. You must enclose $1.00.

ask for: Fishing Fun for Kids Coloring Book

write to: Kid's Fishing
P.O. Box FSK
Future Fishermen Foundation
One Berkley Drive
Spirit Lake, IA 51360

YOU CAN DO IT

fun, fun, fun

This great activity book includes puzzles, facts, cartoons, recipes, mazes, games, and craft and activity ideas. Over forty fun things in all!

directions:	Use paper and an envelope. You must enclose a long, self-addressed, stamped envelope.
ask for:	Kids' Fun Pak
write to:	Kids' Fun Pak The Children's Museum 533 Sixteenth Street Bettendorf, IA 52722

play clay day?

Gloomy outside? It might be a play clay day! Have hours of fun with clay you make with baking soda and other common ingredients. This foldout shows you how to make jewelry, ornaments, and more.

directions:	Use paper and an envelope. You must enclose a long, self-addressed, stamped envelope.
ask for:	How to Make Play Clay
write to:	Play Clay Arm & Hammer Division Church & Dwight Co., Inc. P.O. Box 7648-FS Princeton, NJ 08543-7648

the nose knows

Bring the aroma of spring or Christmas to your room with potpourri. Enough in each packet to make two or three sachets, or one closet ball.

directions: Use paper and an envelope. You must enclose $1.00 for **each** packet.

ask for:
- Greenfield (springtime meadows fragrance)
- Christmas (bayberry, pine fragrance)

write to: Potpourri
Gift Club
P.O. Box 1 MCK
Stony Point, NY 10980

get crafty

Find out all about different crafts with these information-filled booklets about flower making, flower drying, crochet, decorative painting, plaster craft, counted cross stitch, ribbon craft, and macrame.

directions: Use paper and an envelope. You must enclose $1.00.

ask for: Craft Booklets

write to: Craft Booklets
Gift Club
P.O. Box 1 MCB
Stony Point, NY 10980

crafty creatures

With a tug and a twist, turn a tube of yarn into one of six adorable pom pom creatures. Give them to friends or start your own collection. Chose one.

directions: Use paper and an envelope. You must enclose $1.00.

ask for: Pom Pom Friends

write to: Pom Pom Friends
Gift Club
P.O. Box 1
Stony Point, NY 10980

quick! get it!

Quickpoint is a different type of needlepoint. This quickpoint kit comes with canvas, yarn, needle, and instructions.

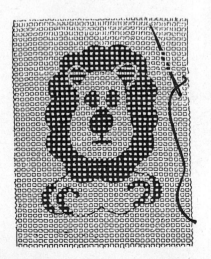

directions: Use paper and an envelope. You must enclose $1.00.

ask for: Quick Point Kit

write to: Quick Point Kit
Gift Club
P.O. Box 1 MCK
Stony Point, NY 10980

latch onto these pennants

Baseball fans will love displaying these Major League latch-hook pennants. You receive yarn, very easy instructions, and the fun of making one yourself. Ask for the Major League team of your choice.

directions: Use paper and an envelope. You must enclose $2.00.

ask for: Latch Hook Baseball Pennants (specify team of choice)

write to: Latch Hook Baseball Pennants
Gift Club
P.O. Box 1
Stony Point, NY 10980

count your stitches

Counted cross stitch is a simple and fun way to make pictures or even spell out words on cloth. This kit includes material, yarn, needle, and instructions.

directions: Use paper and an envelope. You must enclose $1.00.

ask for: Counted Cross Stitch Kit

write to: Counted Cross Stitch Kit
Gift Club
P.O. Box 1 MCK
Stony Point, NY 10980

be an artist

Explore your painting talent with six wooden-handled, camel-hair brushes. You can use these brushes of assorted sizes with water colors, oils, acrylics, stains, and varnish.

directions: Use paper and an envelope. You must enclose $1.00.

ask for: Artist Paintbrushes

write to: Artist Paintbrushes
Giftclub
P.O. Box 1
Stony Point, NY 10980

speak silently

You can talk without making a sound. It's no trick with sign language. Many hearing-impaired people learn how to communicate using the same manual alphabet you get on this card and button.

directions: Use paper and an envelope. You must enclose $1.00 for the button **and** a long, self-addressed, stamped envelope.

ask for: • Manual Alphabet Card (Free)
• Manual Alphabet Button ($1.00)

write to: Keep Quiet
P.O. Box 361
Stanhope, NJ 07874

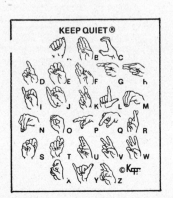

neat idea!

Make cool toys out of things that you have around the house with these idea sheets.

directions: Use paper and an envelope. You must enclose 50¢ for **each** sheet you order.

ask for: Balloon and Funnel Pump Idea Sheet
- Tin Can Pump Idea Sheet
- Making Large Bubbles Idea Sheet
- Special Bubble Machine Idea Sheet
- Pie Plate Water Wheel Idea Sheet
- Raceways: Experiments with Marbles and Tracks Idea Sheet
- Spinning Top That Writes Idea Sheet
- Building Blocks from Milk Cartons Idea Sheet
- Siphon Bottles Idea Sheet
- Explorations with Food Coloring Idea Sheet
- Stained Glass Cookies Idea Sheet
- Making Simple Books Idea Sheet
- Organdy Screening Idea Sheet

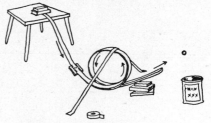

write to: Children's Museum Shop
300 Congress Street
Boston, MA 02210
Attn: Idea Sheets

© 1974
THE CHILDREN'S MUSEUM

they rule!

These just might be the 2 best rulers in the world. When you move them, the dinosaurs show their skeletons and the space monsters rock and roll. They both register inches and centimeters, have a multiplication table, and a place to record personal information. You get both.

directions: Use paper and an envelope. You must enclose $1.50 for **both** rulers.

ask for: Wiggle Ruler Set

write to: Neetstuff
Dept. N-97
P.O. Box 207
Glenside, PA 19038

skatosaurus

A coloring and activity book that features roller-skating dinosaurs. Learn about the benefits of roller-skating and get a 2-for-1 discount coupon good at your local RSA roller-skating rink.

directions: Use paper and an envelope. You must enclose $1.00.

ask for: Roller Skating Fun!

write to: Roller Skating Associations
P.O. Box 81846
Lincoln, NE 68501

checkmate!

Chess has a long, rich history. Most historians believe it was invented about 1,300 years ago in India. Today the game continues to fascinate everyone who enjoys an exciting mental challenge. This 16-page booklet gives 10 tips on winning strategies.

directions: Use paper and an envelope. You must enclose a long, self-addressed, stamped envelope.

ask for: Ten Tips to Winning Chess

write to: Barbara A. DeMaro
U.S. Chess Federation
186 Route 9W
New Windsor, NY 12550

check it out

Chess can be more than just a game with a friend. You can even play by mail! Send for this pamphlet to find out how to get involved with the U.S. Chess Federation and the world of chess.

directions: Use paper and an envelope. You must enclose a long, self-addressed, stamped envelope.

ask for: Be a Winner Pamphlet

write to: Barbara A. DeMaro
U.S. Chess Federation
186 Route 9W
New Windsor, NY 12550

making music

Beautiful music comes in small packages. This guide teaches you how to play one of the world's smallest and most popular instruments—the harmonica.

directions: Use paper and an envelope. You must enclose a long, self-addressed, stamped envelope.

ask for: How to Play the Hohner Harmonica

write to: Hohner, Inc.
Department FD
P.O. Box 9375
Richmond, VA 23227-5035

music's mighty mite

The harmonica was invented about 5,000 years ago in China. Discover its history in *A Brief History of the Harmonica.* Or ask for *Easyreeding* for more harmonica trivia.

directions: Use paper and an envelope. You must enclose a long, self-addressed, stamped envelope for **each** booklet.

ask for: • A Brief History of the Harmonica
• Easyreeding

write to: Hohner, Inc.
Department FD
P.O. Box 9375
Richmond, VA 23227-5035

can you kazoo?

You don't have to study music to play the kazoo, just hum through the big end! This is the original do-it-yourself instrument, and you can have your very own unbreakable, brightly colored Hohner kazoo.

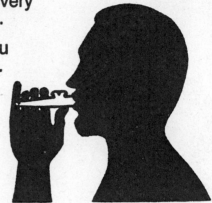

directions: Use paper and an envelope. You must enclose $1.00 for postage.

ask for: Hohner Kazoo

write to: Hohner, Inc.
Department KZ
P.O. Box 9375
Richmond, VA 23227-5035

hanging harmony

Do you have an interest in harmonicas? Or maybe just a blank spot on your wall? Either way, you'll enjoy this giant, full-color poster featuring many kinds of mouth harps.

directions: Use paper and an envelope. You must enclose $1.00.

ask for: Hohner Harmonicas Information Poster.

write to: Hohner, Inc.
P.O. Box 9375
Dept. HPJK
Richmond, VA 23227-5035

pocket piano

Surprise your friends by playing a song on this two-octave mini piano pencil box. It also has its own songbook. With just a touch, the electronic keyboard will play your favorite tunes.

directions:	Use paper and an envelope. You must enclose $2.00.
ask for:	Mini Piano Pencil Box
write to:	Premiums, Promotions, Purchases, Ltd. P.O. Box 460 W. Babylon, NY 11702

mobile memories

Carry your favorite pictures, stickers, and love notes everywhere you go. You get two small photo albums with spaces for 12 snapshots each.

directions:	Use paper and an envelope. You must enclose $1.00.
ask for:	Mini Photo Album
write to:	Mini Photo Album Gift Club P.O. Box 1 Stony Point, NY 10980

STICKERS, STAMPS, AND STUFF

36 STICKERS

save the humans!

For years humans have been trying to save the whale, but the whales on this colored bumper sticker think someone should save the humans!

directions: Use paper and an envelope. You must enclose 75¢ **and** a long, self-addressed, stamped envelope.

ask for: Save the Humans Bumper Sticker

write to: The Wishing Stone
R.D. 3, P.O. Box 208
Washington, NJ 07882

love bug rides again

Deck out your notebooks, or anything else, with these five company symbol stickers.

directions: Use paper and an envelope. You must enclose a long, self-addressed, stamped envelope.

ask for: 5 VW Stickers

write to: Attn: Public Relations/VW Stickers
Volkswagen of America, Inc.
888 W. Big Beaver
Troy, MI 48007-3951

shiny stickers

These shimmering hearts, ice cream cones, and pinwheels will add extra sparkle and shine to your sticker collection. You get two sets of stickers.

directions: Use paper and an envelope. You must enclose $1.00 **and** a long, self-addressed, stamped envelope.

ask for: Rainbow Sticker Cards

write to: Mr. Rainbows
Department K-5
P.O. Box 27056
Philadelphia, PA 19118

prism stickers

Make your day happy with one of these colorful stickers. Put one on your notebook, your shirt, or even your friends. Get 10 shiny-bright stickers per sheet.

directions: Use paper and an envelope. You must enclose $1.00 for **each** sheet.

ask for: Prism Stickers

write to: Expressions
Department FSK
1880 Flatiron Ct.
Boulder, CO 80301

super stickers

Choose some of these sparkling stickers for your collection. Each set includes at least two 3-by-4-inch sticker cards with 8 or 9 stickers on each card. With Love Letters you'll receive numbers, letters, and bright red hearts. Exotic Pets offers fish and parrots, while Best Friends includes cats and dogs. Or try Things That Fly: three cards of blimps, hot air balloons, and propeller airplanes. With the Sticker Zoo you may pick out any two types of zoo animals you like: penguins, monkeys, kangaroos, butterflies, bumble bees, turkeys, frogs, bears, hippos, skunks, giraffes, elephants, rabbits, and angel fish.

directions: Use paper and an envelope. You must enclose the correct amount of money **and** a long, self-addressed, stamped envelope.

ask for:
- Love Letters ($1.00 for set of two sticker cards)
- Exotic Pets ($1.00 for set of two cards)
- Best Friends ($1.00 for set of two cards)
- Things That Fly ($1.50 for set of three cards)
- The Sticker Zoo ($1.00 for set of two cards)

write to: Mr. Rainbows
Department K-I-5
P.O. Box 27056
Philadelphia, PA 19118

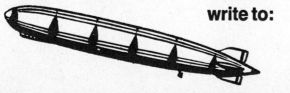

coke 9 ways!

Buvez Coca-Cola! is French for *Drink Coca-Cola.*
This postcard has nine peel-off stickers, each with the
Coke symbol in a different language, including Arabic,
Hebrew, Japanese, Chinese, and Polish.

directions: Use a postcard. (Free)

ask for: Coca-Cola Sticker (limit **one**
card per request)

write to: Consumer Information Center
Department FS
The Coca-Cola Company
P.O. Drawer 1734
Atlanta, GA 30301

holy holograms, batman!

Dazzle your friends with your own hologram decals.
When the sunlight hits them, watch the rainbow 3-D
effect! You get four decals.

directions: Use paper and an envelope. You
must enclose $1.00 **and** a long,
self-addressed, stamped envelope.

ask for: Hologram decals

write to: Neetstuf
Dept. N-96
P.O. Box 207
Glenside, PA 19038

40
STAMPS

stamp collecting

Collecting stamps is fun, and now you can send away for this packet telling you how to start a collection. It even includes 20 international stamps to help you get started.

directions: Use paper and an envelope. You must enclose a long, self-addressed, stamped envelope.

ask for: Beginning Stamp Collector's Packet

write to: Junior Philatelists of America
P.O. Box 1600-FS
Trenton, NJ 08607

fun with stamps

The Junior Philatelists of America is a club for kids who like to collect stamps. Send for a newsletter to learn all the latest information on stamp collecting.

directions: Use paper and an envelope. You must enclose $1.00 **and** a long, self-addressed, stamped envelope.

ask for: Philatelic Observer Sample Newsletter

write to: Junior Philatelists of America
P.O. Box 1600-FS
Trenton, NJ 08607

Nature Stamps

Here are 100 different oversized, beautiful foreign stamps, each depicting a different scene from nature.

directions: Use paper and an envelope. You must enclose $2.00.

ask for: Nature Stamps

write to: Nature Stamps
P.O. Box 466K
Port Washington, NY 11050

heads up

Party down with these 10-inch mylar muppet balloons. Long-lasting, they can be used again and again. Your choice of Miss Piggy, Cookie Monster, Big Bird, Kermit, or Bert and Ernie.

directions: Use paper and an envelope. You must enclose $1.00 for **each** balloon or $4.50 for all five **and** a long, self-addressed, stamped envelope.

ask for: Sesame Street Balloons

write to: Neetstuf
Department N-93
P.O. Box 207
Glenside, PA 19038

unique-corn!

A beautiful postcard of a glamorous white unicorn prancing across a glittery night sky.

directions:	Use paper and an envelope. You must enclose $1.00.
ask for:	The Most Beautiful Postcard in the World
write to:	Expressions 1880 Flatiron Ct. Dept. PC Boulder, CO 80301

third dimension

You don't need special glasses to enjoy this fabulous 3-D photo. The new technology will amaze you! Get a free photo and a brochure about 3-D photography.

directions:	Use paper and an envelope. You must enclose $1.25 **and** a large (8 1/2-by-11-inch), self-addressed, stamped envelope.
ask for:	3-D Photo
write to:	3-D Camera of Minnesota 920 Westwood Lane Dept. FS Anoka, MN 55303

laces—and a whole lot more

What can you do with a dozen colorful shoelaces? Use them for making bracelets, crafts, and more!

directions: Use paper and an envelope. You must enclose $1.00.

ask for: Shoelaces

write to: Shoelaces
Giftclub
P.O. Box 1
Stony Point, NY 10980

glow laces

Would you like your shoes to glow in the dark? When you put these laces under a light for 15 minutes and turn off the light—they shine! Fluorescent fun that keeps you safe too! Use them over and over again.

directions: Use paper and an envelope. You must enclose a long, self-addressed, stamped envelope **and** $1.25 for 5 feet, **or** $2.00 for 10 feet of Glow Laces.

ask for: Shoes Shine

write to: Neetstuf
Dept. N-91
P.O. Box 207
Glenside, PA 19038

picture this

Add a little magnetism to your life! Have a favorite photo mounted on button magnets. Then stick 'em on the refrigerator, in a school locker, anywhere!

directions: Use paper and an envelope. You must enclose a long, self-addressed, stamped envelope **and** $1.00 **and** a photo.

ask for: Photo Magnet Button

write to: Professor Bob
135 Echo Drive
Chambersburg, PA 17201

funny photo contest

Meadowbrook Press is going to publish a book called *The Funniest Family Snapshots* and needs funny photos. If you send one in and it gets used you'll get: $25, the photographer's name in the book, and a chance to win first prize of $1000 and seven other cash prizes, plus a free copy of the book!

directions: Use paper and an envelope. You must enclose a long, self-addressed, stamped envelope **and** your full address and phone number on a piece of paper **and** your photos.

write to: Funny Photo Contest
Meadowbrook Press
18318 Minnetonka Blvd.
Deephaven, MN 55391

switched on

Brighten your room with any one of these cheery, wooden switchplates. Choose from an elephant, a bear, or one of two clowns.

directions: Use paper and an envelope. You must enclose $1.00 for **each** switchplate.

ask for: Children's Switchplate Cover

write to: Switchplate Cover
Gift Club
P.O. Box 1
Stony Point, NY 10980

under the rainbow

Don't let things slide. Use these strong rainbow magnets to hold up your important memos on any metal surface. You get a set of three.

directions: Use paper and an envelope. You must enclose $1.00 **and** a long, self-addressed, stamped envelope.

ask for: Rainbow Magnets

write to: Mr. Rainbows
Dept. 90-6
P.O. Box 27056
Philadelphia, PA 19118

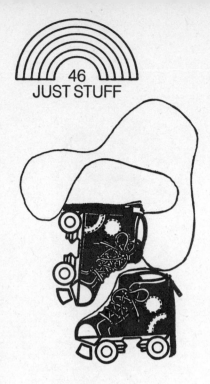

sporty purse

Keep your change in a roller skate. This multi-colored vinyl purse looks like a little roller skate, but it has a zipper and room for coins or other stuff you need to take with you.

directions: Use paper and an envelope. You must enclose $1.00.

ask for: Roller Skate Coin Purse

write to: Eleanor Curran
Department FS
530 Leonard Street
Brooklyn, NY 11222

brace yourself

Make a special "friendship bracelet" for your best buddy. This kit includes special colored string and instructions for creating the latest fashion rage!

directions: Use a letter and an envelope. You must enclose $1.00.

ask for: Friendship Bracelet

write to: Friendship Bracelet
Gift Club
P.O. Box 1
Stony Point, NY 10980

framing fun

Here are two colorful key chains that also double as picture frames when you insert your favorite photo. These 2-by-2-inch frames are made of colorful, durable plastic.

directions: Use paper and an envelope. You must enclose $1.00 **and** a long, self-addressed, stamped envelope. Please *do not* send photographs.

ask for: Picture Frame Key Chains

write to: Mr. Rainbows
Department P-1
P.O. Box 27056
Philadelphia, PA 19118

who's got the button?

Send in your favorite snapshot and have it made into a button just for you. Wear it on your shirt, jacket, or cap. Great as a gift too.

directions: Use paper and an envelope. You must enclose $1.00, a nonreturnable photo, **and** a long, self-addressed, stamped envelope.

ask for: Photo Button

write to: Tony Hsieh
Dept FSFK
28 Coast Oak Way
San Rafael, CA 94903

really radical reptiles

Everyone loves these neon-bright, inflatable dinosaurs. Each is over a foot tall, and they come in many different varieties. So start collecting them today!

directions: Use paper and an envelope. You must enclose $2.00.

ask for: Inflatable Dinosaur

write to: Eleanor Curran
530 Leonard Street
Dept. D
Brooklyn, NY 11222

READIN' 'RITIN', AND 'RITHMETIC

young imaginations

Explore these exciting magazines with your parents or by yourself.

- *Turtle* (ages 2 to 5) is a unique magazine filled with read-to-me stories, hidden pictures, dot-to-dots, coloring pages, and more.
- *Humpty Dumpty's* (ages 4 to 6) entertains and teaches with fun stories, poems, puzzles, and crafts.
- *Children's Playmate* (ages 6 to 8) offers colorfully illustrated stories for beginning readers, intriguing puzzles, games, recipes, cartoons, and activities.

directions: Use paper and an envelope. You must enclose $1.00 for **each** magazine requested.

ask for:
- Turtle Magazine
- Humpty Dumpty's Magazine
- Children's Playmate Magazine

write to: Roanita Milton, Samples
Children's Better Health Institute
P.O. Box 567
Indianapolis, IN 46206

young adventurers

These three magazines for older readers invite you to learn, laugh, and create.

- *Jack and Jill* (ages 7 to 10) continues to entertain with illustrated fiction, jokes, activities—plus works by kids like you.
- *Child Life* (ages 9 to 11) offers Diane's Dinosaur comics, Odd Job career profiles, activities, and great stories.
- *Children's Digest* (ages 10 to 12) features contemporary fiction, articles on important issues, challenging puzzles, book reviews, and cartoons.

directions: Use paper and an envelope. You must enclose $1.00 for **each** magazine requested.

ask for:
- Jack and Jill Magazine
- Children's Digest Magazine
- Child Life Magazine

write to: Roanita Milton, Samples
Children's Better Health Institute
P.O. Box 567
Indianapolis, IN 46206

fun-filled catalog

You won't believe the strange and comical items you'll find in this catalog! Nearly 2,000 jokes and tricks, sport and hobby items, books, electronic gadgets, and novelties are listed. Recommended for ages ten and up.

directions: Use paper and an envelope. You must send 25¢.

ask for: The Things You Never Knew Existed Catalog

write to: Johnson Smith Co.
Dept M-405
P.O. Box 25500
Bradenton, FL 34206-5500

better buys

Here's a catalog of 200 free and low-cost consumer publications from the federal government. They can teach you about cars, food, health, medicine, and much more. Use them for school reports!

directions: Use a postcard. (Free)

ask for: The Consumer Information Catalog

write to: Free Catalog
Pueblo, CO 81009

it's story time

Listen to two exciting stories on this 60-minute storytime cassette. Side one is "Yellow Jack, the Giant Killer: The Story of Dr. Walter Reed," and the second side is an exciting Western adventure.

directions: Use paper and an envelope. You must enclose $1.00.

ask for: Yellow Jack Cassette

write to: Your Story Hour
P.O. Box 15
Berrien Springs, MI 49103

all-righta!

Make up great stories with this fun refrigerator game from Ore-Ida. It's perfect for rainy days or long car rides.

directions: Use paper and an envelope. You must enclose $1.00 **and** your name and address.

ask for: Ore-Ida Story Starter Game

write to: Ore-Ida Story Starter Game
P.O. Box 8004
Clinton, IA 52736

pet care bookmarks

Mark your place with bookmarks from the Animal Protection Institute of America. Read about the eating, sleeping, and bathing habits of cats, dogs, and birds, and learn how to take care of them. Get all three.

directions: Use paper and an envelope. You must enclose a long, self-addressed, stamped envelope.

ask for: Free Animal Bookmarks

write to: Animal Protection Institute
Free Animal Bookmark Offer
P.O. Box 22505
Sacramento, CA 95822

wrist writing

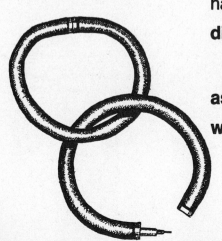

You can always have a pen at an arm's length with this handy pen bracelet.

directions: Use paper and an envelope. You must enclose $1.00 **and** a long, self-addressed, stamped envelope.

ask for: Pen Bracelet

write to: Neetstuf
Dept. N-3
P.O. Box 207
Glenside, PA 19038

lovely letters

This beautiful stationery has been prepared especially for kids by kids. You get 3 sheets of multi-colored stationery with matching envelopes all designed by two teenage girls.

directions: Use paper and a envelope. You must enclose 50¢ **and** a long, self-addressed, stamped envelope.

ask for: Sponge-Works Stationery

write to: Sponge-Works Stationery
448 Collings Avenue
Collingswood, NJ 08107

mail up a storm

Wake up your postman with this assortment of 50 envelopes in shades and sizes galore.

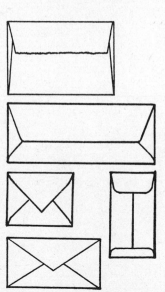

directions: Use paper and an envelope. You must enclose $1.00.

ask for: Assorted Envelope Package

write to: Assorted Envelope Package
Gift Club
P.O. Box 1
Stony Point, NY 10980

be a pen pal

Pen pals are special friends. Send for a free *Student Letter Exchange* order form (pen pals cost $1 each and you have to order two, but don't send any money yet!). You can ask for a pen pal from almost any foreign country and any state in the United States (ages 10-22).

directions:	Use paper and an envelope. You must enclose a long, self-addressed, stamped envelope.
ask for:	Student Letter Exchange Order Form
write to:	Student Letter Exchange 215 5th Avenue S.E. Waseca, MN 56093

sign here, please

To start your collection of autographs, send for this list of TV stars like Linda Evans from "Dynasty," movie stars like Harrison Ford, and singers like Michael Jackson. You get a list of 35 names and addresses.

directions:	Use paper and an envelope. You must enclose 50¢ **and** a long, self addressed,stamped envelope
ask for:	Autograph Address List
write to:	Autograph Address List Collectors Club Department FSK P.O. Box 467 Rockville Center, NY 11571-0467

write on!

Write your next letter on this colored stationery.
Includes 15 matching pieces of paper and envelopes.

directions: Use paper and an envelope. You must enclose $1.00.

ask for: Stationery

write to: Stationery Gift Club
P.O. Box 1 MST
Stony Point, NY 10890

kid's calling cards

These sets of illustrated calling cards have spaces for your name, address, telephone number, or any message you wish to write. Each set includes two cards of six different designs; 12 cards in all!

directions: Use paper and an envelope. You must enclose 75¢ **and** a long, self-addressed, stamped envelope for **each** set. Specify which set you want.

ask for:
- Fantasy Creatures
- Stuffed Toys
- Endangered Species
- Dinosaurs

write to: The Wishing Stone
R.D. 3, P.O. Box 208
Washington, NJ 07882

math in a flash

How can a ruler help you with math? When the ruler has a multiplication table written on it! Tilt the ruler one way and you'll see the problems. Tilt it the other way and you'll see the answers.

directions: Use paper and an envelope. You must enclose a long, self-addressed, stamped envelope **and** $1.00.

ask for: Just-A-Twist Ruler

write to: IPM
Department M
P.O. Box 1181
Hammond, IN 46325

perplexing puzzles

If you like word games, take a crack at solving some of Professor Pinkerton's most perplexing puzzles. You get a "Can You Solve the Mystery" sticker as well.

directions: Use paper and an envelope. You must enclose 25¢ **and** a long, self-addressed, stamped envelope.

ask for: Perplexing Puzzles Pamphlet

write to: Meadowbrook Press
Department PP/CYSM
18318 Minnetonka Blvd.
Deephaven, MN 55391

MEADOWBROOK

59

U.S. MAIL

HEALTHY AND WISE

recycling at home

You can help save our planet. Learn how to recycle by reading this pamphlet from the Ohio Department of Natural Resources. (For other offers from the ODNR see page 74.)

directions: Use paper and an envelope. You must enclose a long, self-addressed, stamped envelope.

ask for: Recycling at Home

write to: Publications Center
Ohio Department of Natural Resources
4383 Fountain Square Drive
Columbus, OH 43224

sun power

Learn all about sun power and other forms of safe and clean energy. The Conservation and Renewable Energy Inquiry Referral Service (CAREIRS) has two fact sheets to send you about renewable energy.

directions: Use a postcard or call 1-800-523-2929. (Free)

ask for:
- Solar Energy and You—FS118
- Learning About Renewable Energy—FS119

write to: CAREIRS
P.O. Box 8900
Silver Spring, MD 20704

safety first

Learn how to take good care of your bicycle, ride safely, and other safe habits. Choose any two.

directions: Use paper and an envelope. You must include a long, self-addressed, stamped envelope.

ask for:
- Bicycle Safety Pamphlet
- Play It Safe
- Tuffy Talks About Medicine

write to: Aetna Life & Casualty
Corporate Communications DA/23
151 Farmington Avenue
Hartford, CT 06156

kinderprint i.d.

Make a record of your fingerprints for easy identification with this easy-to-use print strip. There's a place for your photo and your description—and you also get a balloon.

directions: Use paper and an envelope. You must enclose $1.00 **and** a long, self-addressed, stamped envelope.

ask for: Kinderprint Kit I.D. Record

write to: Special Products
Department FS
47 McClellan
Amsterdam, NY 12010

YES,
I MIND
IF YOU
SMOKE

take a deep breath

You might know that you need your lungs to breathe, but what else do you know? The American Lung Association makes learning fun with a coloring book, a crossword puzzle, and two activity books.

directions: Use a postcard. (Free)

ask for:
- **#0840** No Smoking Lungs at Work Activity Book
- **#0071** Let's Solve the Smokeword Puzzle
- **#0250** Don't You Dare Breathe That Air Activity Book
- **#0043** No Smoking Coloring Book

write to: American Lung Association
GPO Box #596-RB
New York, NY 10019

no smoking!

This stop-sign-shaped sign might keep people from smoking when you hang it up. It warns: *Lungs at Work No Smoking.*

directions: Use a postcard. (Free)

ask for: **#0121** Lungs at Work Sign

write to: American Lung Association
GPO Box #596-RB
New York, NY 10001

LUNGS
AT WORK
NO SMOKING
AMERICAN
LUNG
ASSOCIATION

smoky villain

This full-color comic book stars Spider-Man and other super heroes who battle the villain, Smokescreen. It's full of action. Read it and see how smoking affects your health and life—for the worse.

directions: Use a postcard. (Free)

ask for: Spider-Man Comic Book

write to: Your local American Cancer Society office. It's listed in the telephone book.

tin grins are in!

Learn about orthodontics. Send for this newsletter about wearing braces.

directions: Use a postcard. (Free)

ask for: Smile of Health newsletter

write to: American Association of Orthodontists Department KD 460 N. Lindbergh Blvd. St. Louis, MO 63141

dealing with cancer

Having a brother or sister with cancer can be hard for you too. You might be confused about your thoughts or feelings. Reading this 16-page booklet could help you feel better.

directions: Use a postcard. (Free)

ask for: When Your Brother or Sister Has Cancer

write to: Your local American Cancer Society office. It's listed in the telephone book.

bucket brigade

Glue this red, white, and blue label to a one-pound coffee can to make an emergency fire pail. Filled with baking soda, the pail is ready for any electrical or grease fire. Includes instructions and a fire chart.

directions: Use paper and an envelope. You must enclose a long, self-addressed, stamped envelope.

ask for: Fire Pail Label

write to: Fire Pail
Arm & Hammer Division
Church & Dwight Co., Inc.
P.O. Box 7648-FS
Princeton, NJ 08543-7648

great ideas

Baking soda isn't just for baking! It can be used to freshen the air, put out fires, and much more. Send for this pamphlet to find out all about baking soda.

directions: Use paper and an envelope. You must enclose a long, self-addressed, stamped envelope.

ask for: Great Ideas Pamphlet

write to: Great Ideas
Arm & Hammer Division
Church & Dwight Co., Inc.
P.O. Box 7648-FS
Princeton, NJ 08543-7648

looking good

How can baking soda keep you healthy? Use it instead of toothpaste, as a mouthwash, and much more. This pamphlet tells you all about baking-soda health care.

directions: Use paper and an envelope. You must enclose a long, self-addressed, stamped envelope.

ask for: Looking Good Pamphlet

write to: Looking Good
Arm & Hammer Division
Church & Dwight Co., Inc.
P.O. Box 7648-FS
Princeton, NJ 08543-7648

rice is nice

Learn how climate and terrain combine to produce top-quality rice in California and some Southern states. Send for more facts about rice, a pamphlet of recipes, and a fun activity booklet.

directions: Use paper and an envelope. You must enclose a long, self-addressed, stamped envelope for **each** item.

ask for:
- Facts About U.S. Rice
- Cooking Healthy with Rice
- Teaching the Fun Way...with Rice!

write to: (Name of Brochure)
The Rice Council
P.O. Box 740123
Houston, TX 77274

jolly good time

Make a perfect popcorn ball without burning your fingers or getting them sticky. Send for this red plastic popcorn-ball maker and Jolly Time's collection of homemade family recipes, too.

directions: Use paper and an envelope. You must enclose $1.00.

ask for: Jolly Time Pop Corn Ball Maker

write to: Jolly Time Pop Corn
American Pop Corn Company
P.O. Box 178, Department H
Sioux City, IA 51102

MEADOWBROOK

67

U.S.
MAIL

ANIMAL KINGDOM

wide world of animals

Did you know that a baby whale drinks up to 25 gallons of milk a day, or that zebras have stripes to help them hide in tall grass? Discover the fascinating world of animals in this 16-page book full of stories, games, facts, and fun.

directions: Use paper and an envelope. You must enclose $1.00.

ask for: Best of Animalia

write to: MSPCA—Humane Education Department of Circulation 350 S. Huntington Avenue Boston, MA 02130

living with animals

Go for a day to the zoo and a farm to find out about pets and people. Discover the world of animals in the 14 stories in this illustrated book.

directions: Use paper and an envelope. You must enclose $1.00.

ask for: Living with Animals Storybook

write to: MSPCA—Humane Education Department of Circulation 350 S. Huntington Avenue Boston, MA 02130

attack and defense

Send for this colorful "Attack and Defense" poster that features a bear, a skunk, an elk, and some reptiles as they prepare to attack or defend themselves.

directions: Use paper and an envelope. You must enclose $1.00.

ask for: Attack and Defense Poster

write to: P. Moreland
Anniston Museum of Natural History
P.O. Box 1587
Anniston, AL 36202

elsa and her friends

Elsa Clubs of America are devoted to educating people about the world's endangered wildlife. Send for a colorful bumper sticker or badge (or both).

directions: Use paper and an envelope. You must enclose $1.00 for **each** item.

ask for: • Born Free Bumper Sticker
• Born Free Badge

write to: Born Free
P.O. Box 4572-X
North Hollywood, CA 91607

70
HOUSEPETS

caring for cats and dogs

From feeding to first aid, these booklets provide the information a cat or dog owner needs. Each is filled with good advice that should please your pet.

directions: Use paper and an envelope. You must enclose $1.00 for **each** booklet.

ask for:
- Care of Cats Booklet
- Care of Dogs Booklet

write to: MSPCA—Humane Education Department of Circulation 350 S. Huntington Avenue Boston, MA 02130

animal first aid

If you care about animals and like to help them, this 21-page guide is for you. It teaches basic animal first aid, from how to approach an injured animal to setting broken legs.

directions: Use paper and an envelope. You must enclose $1.00.

ask for: Angell Memorial Guide to Animal First Aid

write to: MSPCA—Humane Education Department of Circulation 350 S. Huntington Avenue Boston, MA 02130

small and furry

Gerbils, mice, rats, rabbits, hamsters, and guinea pigs are fun to watch as they burrow in their nests or nibble on food. Learn about small mammals as pets in this complete 28-page guide.

directions: Use paper and an envelope. You must enclose $1.00.

ask for: Small Mammal Care Booklet

write to: MSPCA—Humane Education
Department of Circulation
350 S. Huntington Avenue
Boston, MA 02130

horsing around

Are you a horse lover? Then you'll love "The Story of Harness Racing," a coloring book illustrating the history of this equestrian sport. You can also get one copy of the U.S. Trotting Association's magazine, "Hoofbeats."

directions: Use a postcard. (Free)

ask for: • The Story of Harness Racing
• Hoofbeats

write to: US Trotting Association
Attn: Coloring Book Dept.
750 Michigan Ave.
Columbus, OH 43215

high steppers

Learn about these high-stepping horses through the American Saddlebred Horse Association. The coloring poster and full-color brochures will show you this beautiful horse in action.

directions: Use paper and an envelope. You must enclose $1.00.

ask for: Coloring Poster, Brochures, and Sticker

write to: ASHA
Department S
4093 Iron Works Pike
Lexington, KY 40511

the golden horse

Since humans first domesticated the horse, the palomino, or the golden horse, has been highly prized by emperors, kings, and queens. Send for a full-color brochure about this prizewinner.

directions: Use paper and an envelope. You must enclose 50¢ **and** a long, self-addressed, stamped envelope.

ask for: Invest in Gold Brochure

write to: Palomino Horse Breeders of America, Inc.
Department FS
15253 E. Skelly Drive
Tulsa, OK 74116-2620

the quarter horse

Learn more about the beautiful, athletic American Quarter Horse and the American Junior Quarter Horse Association, a fun organization which kids can join.

directions: Use paper and an envelope. You must enclose the correct amount of money.

ask for:
- American Junior Quarter Horse Association Booklet (Free)
- For You, AQH Booklet (Free)
- AQH Coloring Book (50¢)
- AQH Activity/Puzzles Book ($1.00)

write to: AQHA
Department FS
P.O. Box 200
Amarillo, TX 79168

arabians—riding proud

This hardy breed originated in the Arabian desert. These pamphlets and wall chart will tell you more.

directions: Use paper and an envelope. You must enclose the correct amount of money.

ask for:
- Arabian Horse Pamphlet (Free)
- Half-Arabian/Anglo-Arabian Pamphlet (Free)
- Parts of the Horse Wall Chart ($1.00)

write to: IAHA
P.O. Box 33696
Denver, CO 80233-0696

wildlife wisdom

Did you know that animals rarely abandon their babies? Learn about orphaned animals, fishing, and building bluebird houses in these three pamphlets by the Ohio Department of Natural Resources.

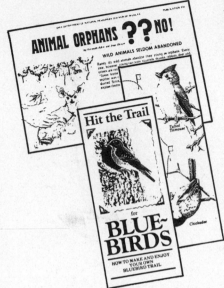

directions: Use paper and an envelope. You must enclose a long, self-addressed, stamped envelope.

ask for:
- Hit the Trail for Bluebirds
- Animal Orphans? No!
- Fishing FUNdamentals

write to: Publications Center
Ohio Department of Natural Resources
4383 Fountain Square Drive
Columbus, OH 43224

animal poster

This large coloring poster is filled with people and animals living happily together in homes, at the zoo, on the farm, and in the woods.

directions: Use paper and an envelope. You must enclose 50¢.

ask for: Living with Animals Poster

write to: MSPCA—Humane Education
Department of Circulation
350 S. Huntington Avenue
Boston, MA 02130

WORLD OF WONDERS

seed power

You and the sun can turn hundreds of carrot and lettuce seeds into a healthy salad.

directions: Use paper and an envelope. You must enclose $1.00.

ask for: Special Kids' Salad Garden Seeds

write to: Butterbrooke Farm
78-K Barry Road
Oxford, CT 06483

watch it grow

All you need is some soil in a sunny spot, patience, and cooperation from Mother Nature. Send for this collection of vegetable seeds, plus two different kinds of flower seeds.

directions: Use paper and an envelope. You must enclose $1.00.

ask for: A Child's Garden Seed Collection

write to: Watch It Grow
3670 Enterprise Ave.
Hayward, CA 94545

this land is our land

Our government is concerned about two of our most important resources—water and soil. These pamphlets tell you what you need to know so you can help conserve what we now enjoy.

- **Flood Plain Management**—This illustrated pamphlet discusses how to prevent flooding and the resulting damage.
- **Conservation and the Water Cycle**—This pamphlet presents a colored picture of how hydrologic processes effect the earth and its inhabitants.
- **Grass Makes Its Own Food**—This illustrated pamphlet explains how this "taken for granted" plant grows.
- **Going Wild with Soil and Water Conservation**—This 24-page colorful booklet describes many soil and water conservation practices that can benefit wildlife.

directions: Use paper and an envelope. You must enclose a long, self-addressed, stamped envelope.

ask for: Name of pamphlet

write to: U.S. Department of Agriculture
Soil Conservation Service
Room 0054-S
P.O. Box 2890
Washington, DC 20013

save with soda

You can use soda in ways that save money and the environment. Read this brochure to find out how baking soda can be a better alternative for common household products.

directions: Use paper and an envelope. You must enclose a long, self-addressed, stamped envelope.

ask for: Environmental Brochure

write to: Arm & Hammer Consumer Relations P.O. Box Box 7648 ENV Princeton, NJ 08543-7648

save a stream

This stream-watcher's guide teaches you how to tell if a stream is healthy or not.

directions: Use paper and an envelope. You must enclose a long, self-addressed, stamped envelope.

ask for: Save Our Streams Packet

write to: Save Our Streams Packet Izaak Walton League of America Level B 1401 Wilson Blvd. Arlington, VA 22209

sunny side up

If you're interested in solar energy activities, send for these instructions on how to build a solar-powered hot dog cooker.

directions: Use paper and an envelope. You must enclose 25¢ **and** a long, self-addressed, stamped envelope.

ask for: Solar Hot Dog Cooker Directions

write to: Energy Management Center
P.O. Box 190
9130 Old Post Road
Port Richey, FL 34673

what's the weather?

Instead of asking "how's the weather?" ask *"what's the weather?"* This pamphlet tells you facts about average temperatures, different cloud types, and how the weather affects passenger jets.

directions: Use paper and an envelope. You must enclose a long, self-addressed, stamped envelope.

ask for: What's the Weather Pamphlet

write to: Air France Distributing Center
NYC DX
2039 9th Avenue
Ronkonkoma, NY 11779

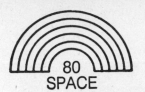

model mania

Be a space cadet and learn all about model rockets. This 64-page, full-color catalog describes rockets you can build and really launch.

directions: Use a postcard. (Free)

ask for: Free Model Rocket Catalog

write to: Estes Industries
Dept. 761
1295 H Street
Penrose, CO 81240

spacemodeling

Discover the fun and challenge of spacemodeling. You can run your own miniature Cape Canaveral and fly any of the hundreds of different models available. Get started by sending for this pamphlet.

directions: Use a postcard. (Free)

ask for: Hobby of Model Rocketry Brochure

write to: National Association of Rocketry
2140 Colburn Drive
Shakopee, MN 55379

MEADOWBROOK

81

U.S.
MAIL

A WORLD
WE MAKE

making paper

With just a few common household items, you'll be in the papermaking business. You won't get rich, but you will have some fun. This brochure tells how.

directions: Use a postcard.

ask for: How You Can Make Paper

write to: How You Can Make Paper
American Paper Institute, Inc.
260 Madison Avenue
New York, NY 10016

paper comes to america

What would you lose if paper was never invented? This book, the funny papers, birthday cards, and a whole lot more! This large poster traces paper's amazing history up to its production in the United States.

directions: Use a postcard.

ask for: How Paper Came to America Poster

write to: How Paper Came to America
American Paper Institute, Inc.
260 Madison Avenue
New York, NY 10016

the paper story

What's So Special About Paper? tells you about careers in the paper industry. *Paper and Paper Manufacture* tells about paper's history, the technology used to produce it, and its environmental impact.

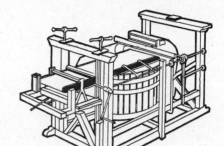

directions: Use a postcard. (Free)

ask for:
- What's So Special About Paper?
- Paper and Paper Manufacture

write to: (Title of booklet requested)
American Paper Institute, Inc.
260 Madison Avenue
New York, NY 10016

the quest for light

From stone-age torches to oil lamps to laser beams, people have always tried to make darkness a little brighter. These three booklets are full of information about the human quest for light.

directions: Use a postcard. (Free)

ask for:
- History of Human Achievement
- Radiant Energy
- Saving Lighting Energy

write to: Barbara Sitzman
GTE Products Corporation
Marketing Services Center
70 Empire Drive
West Seneca, NY 14224

ump's fwat

Who is Ump and what is a fwat? Ump is a caveman and a fwat...well, send for the story of *Ump's Fwat* and find out for yourself. You'll get a 23-page booklet with colorful pictures that will make you laugh. And while you're finding out what a fwat is, you'll learn something about economics!

directions: Use a postcard. (Free)

ask for: Ump's Fwat

write to: Academy for Economic Education
125 Sovran Center
Richmond, VA 23277

money matters

Do you understand inflation? Do you want to know more about coins, banks, and other money matters? The Federal Reserve Bank of New York is offering eight comic books and pamphlets on these topics. Order as many as you want.

85
MONEY

directions: Use a postcard. (Free)

ask for:
- The Story of Consumer Credit (Spanish version available)
- Coins and Currency
- 1989-90 Reading and Viewing
- The Story of Checks and Electronic Payments
- The Story of Foreign Trade and Exchange
- The Story of Inflation
- Too Much, Too Little (origins of the Federal Reserve System)
- The Story of Banks and Thrifts
- Once Upon a Dime
- The Story of Money

write to: Federal Reserve Bank of New York
Public Information Department
33 Liberty Street
New York, NY 10045

famous americans

Listen to stories on tape of Americans who helped make our country great. A nurse, a scientist, a man without a country, a pilot, and more. One story on each side of a sixty-minute tape with realistic sound effects.

directions: Use paper and an envelope. You must enclose $1.00 for **each** tape.

ask for:
- Man Without a Country, Lt. Philip Nolan
- The Spirit of St. Louis, Charles Lindbergh

write to: Your Story Hour
Department FSC
P.O. Box 15
Berrien Springs, MI 49103

a real piece of history

The Civil War is an important part of American history. Now you can have a small piece of that history with this authentic Civil War bullet. This round metal bullet is over 120 years old!

directions: Use paper and an envelope. You must enclose $1.00.

ask for: Authentic Civil War Bullet

write to: National Tower
999 Baltimore Pike
Gettysburg, PA 17325

stars and stripes

Star-Spangled Banner, Old Glory, Stars and Stripes—all are names for the American flag, a flag that's had 27 versions! Want to know more? Send for these three folders.

directions: Use a postcard. (Free)

ask for:
- Etiquette of the Stars and Stripes
- Ten Short Flag Stories
- Questions and Answers on the U.S. Flag

write to: Americanism Director
VFW National Headquarters
34th and Broadway
Kansas City, MO 64111

The Fifth Flag (1820)

history comes alive

It's more fun to study history when you can look at and touch a piece of it. What did the Declaration of Independence really look like? How about the Bill of Rights? Or a poster offering a $25,000 reward for Jesse James—Dead or Alive? Send for these antiqued parchment replicas of historical documents, posters, banknotes, and maps. Each one goes through a secret 11-step process that makes it look and feel old!

directions: Use paper and an envelope. You must enclose $1.00 for **each** set.

ask for: Each set by its name **and** number

write to: Historical Documents Company
Department S
8 N. Preston Street
Philadelphia, PA 19104
Here's a list of historical posters, documents, maps, and banknotes to choose from.

- **#201S** Declaration of Independence **and** the Bill of Rights
  (enclose $1.00)

- **#202S** 14 Different Colonial and Revolutionary War Banknotes
  (enclose $1.00)

PROCLAMATION
OF THE
GOVERNOR OF MISSOURI!

$25,000 REWARD

FRANK JAMES   JESSE JAMES

JESSE JAMES
DEAD OR ALIVE

$15,000 REWARD FOR FRANK JAMES
SIGNED ST. LOUIS MIDLAND RAILROAD & STATE OF MISSOURI

- **#203S** 12 Different Confederate Banknotes (enclose $1.00)

- **#204S** Map of the Voyages of Discovery **and** 1651 World Map (enclose $1.00)

- **#205S** Pirate Treasure Map **and** Pirates' Creed of Ethics (enclose $1.00)

- **#206S** Jesse James **and** Billy the Kid Reward Posters (enclose $1.00)

- **#207S** Civil War Map **and** Revolutionary War Battlefields Map (enclose $1.00)

- **#208S** History of Famous American Flags **and** Pictures of all U.S. Presidents (enclose $1.00)

- **#209S** Lincoln's Gettysburg Address **and** Lincoln's Portrait and Thoughts (enclose $1.00)

- **#2011S** 1776 Continental Dollar Coin **and** 1778 $20 U.S. Continental Banknote (enclose $1.00)

- **#2012S** Constitution **and** Star Spangled Banner (enclose $1.00)

- **#213S** Butch Cassidy **and** the Sundance Kid (enclose $1.00)

what in the world

The National Geographic Society wants to send you a copy of *World*, their children's magazines packed with stunning photos and articles on nature, science, and geography. Special features include posters, maps, "Kids Did It', "Far Out Facts", and more. Send for a free copy and travel the world.

directions: Use a postcard. (Free)

ask for: National Geographic World Sample Copy

write to: National Geographic World
17th and M. Streets NW, Ste. 687
Washington, D.C. 20036

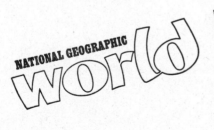

GOING
MY WAY?

family travel guide

Plan your best vacation yet with family travel guides from Carousel Press. You get their catalog and a travel game.

directions: Use paper and an envelope. You must enclose $1.00.

ask for: Family Travel Guide Catalog

write to: Carousel Press
Family Travel Guides
P.O. Box 6061
Albany, CA 94706

fun on the run

Hunting for new car games? This 31-page booklet is filled with games everyone can play—games with signs, colors, sounds, and more.

directions: Use paper and an envelope. You must enclose $1.00 **and** your name and address.

ask for: Travel Games

write to: The Beavers
Department FS
Star Route, P.O. Box 537
Laporte, MN 56461

go with yogi

Get this activity book loaded with puzzles, pictures to color, and word games. You can have fun with Yogi Bear as you travel through Jellystone Park.

directions: Use paper and an envelope. You must enclose 50¢.

ask for: Yogi Bear Travel Activity Book

write to: Skippy Activity Book
Department YB-FS
P.O. Box 307
Coventry, CT 06238

a capital idea

Learn all about Washington, D.C.—the nation's capital. This colorful brochure has information on museums, monuments, transportation, sports, theaters, major annual events and places to stay, as well as maps to help you get around.

directions: Use a postcard. (Free)

ask for: Washington, D.C.: A Capital City! Brochure

write to: Washington, D.C. Convention & Visitors Association
Attn:Tourist Information
1212 New York Ave., N.W.
Washington, D.C. 20005

94
HISTORIC PLACES

historic gettysburg

Gettysburg, Pennsylvania, was the site of the most famous Civil War battle. Today the town remembers and honors that battle with more than 1,000 monuments and other attractions. This 56-page guide tells you about all the sights and about visiting Gettysburg.

directions: Use a postcard. (Free)

ask for: Gettysburg Tourism Booklet

write to: Gettysburg Travel Council
Department 001
35 Carlisle Street
Gettysburg, PA 17325

a wealth of history

The United States has a wealth of history, and numerous U.S. parks and monuments preserve and honor that history. To learn more about some of the most famous historic and natural sites, write to the addresses below.

directions: Use a postcard. (Free)

ask for: Tourism Information

write to: The office with information about the place that interests you.

The Alamo

Texas Tourist Development Agency
P.O. Box 12008
Austin, TX 78711

Death Valley, California

National Park Service Information
Fort Mason, Building 201
Bay and Franklin Streets
San Francisco, CA 94123

California State Parks System
Parks and Recreation
P.O. Box 2390
Sacramento, CA 95811

Grand Canyon

Arizona Office of Tourism
Suite 180
1480 E. Bethany Home Road
Phoenix, AZ 85014

Arizona State Parks
1688 W. Adams
Phoenix, AZ 85007

Mount Rushmore

U.S. Department of Interior
National Park Service
Mt. Rushmore National Memorial
P.O. Box 268
Keystone, SD 55751-0268

Mount Vernon and Monticello

Virginia State Travel Service
Bell Tower
Capitol Square
Richmond, VA 23219

Virginia State Chamber of
Commerce
611 E. Franklin Street
Richmond, VA 23219

Valley Forge

Superintendent
Valley Forge National Historic
Park
Valley Forge, PA 19481

Williamsburg

Director of Travel
Colonial Williamsburg Foundation
P.O. Box C
Williamsburg, VA 23187

land of history

Even though it's one of the world's newest countries, Israel has a history that spans thousands of years. The story of Israel, past and present, is dramatic and interesting. Send for brochures and maps, and discover the story of Israel.

directions: Use a postcard. (Free)

ask for:
- Geography Brochure
- A Letter from Israel Pamphlet
- Israel Ancient and Modern Map
- Masada Pamphlet
- USA and Israel Booklet
- America in Israel Brochure
- The Birth of Two Nations Booklet
- The Flag of Israel Brochure
- Israel—The Land

write to: The office serving your area

Address	Area Served
Embassy of Israel 3514 International Drive NW Washington, DC 20008	District of Columbia, North Carolina, Maryland, Virginia, West Virginia
Consulate General of Israel 1020 Statler Office Building Boston, MA 02116	Massachusetts, Maine, Vermont, New Hampshire, Rhode Island
Consulate General of Israel 800 Second Avenue New York, NY 10017	New York, Connecticut, northern New Jersey, Puerto Rico
Consulate General of Israel 225 S. 15th Street Philadelphia, PA 19102	Pennsylvania, Delaware, Ohio, Kentucky, southern New Jersey
Consulate General of Israel Suite 656 805 Peachtree Street NE Atlanta, GA 30365	Georgia, Alabama, Tennessee, South Carolina, Mississippi

Address	**Areas Served**
Consulate General of Israel 330 Biscayne Blvd., Ste. 510 Miami, FL 33132	Florida
Consulate General of Israel 111 E. Wacker Dr., Ste. 1308 Chicago, IL 60601	Illinois, Minnesota, North Dakota, South Dakota, Wisconsin, Indiana, Iowa, Nebraska, Kansas, Michigan, Missouri
Consulate General of Israel One Greenway Plaza E., Ste. 722 Houston, TX 77046	Texas, Arkansas, Oklahoma, New Mexico, Louisiana
Consulate General of Israel 6380 Wilshire Blvd., Ste. 1700 Los Angeles, CA 90048	Arizona, southern California, Hawaii, Colorado, Nevada, Utah, Wyoming
Consulate General of Israel 220 Bush Street, Ste. 550 San Francisco, CA 94104	Alaska, northern California, Oregon, Washington, Montana, Idaho

discover america with free tourist packets

Whether you're planning a family trip or are just curious about your country, you'll want to send for these state and city tourism packets. Every city and state will send something special.

directions: Use a postcard. (Free)

ask for: Tourism Information

write to: State or city information office of your choice.

Alabama

Bureau of Publicity & Information
State of Alabama
532 S. Perry Street
Montgomery, AL 36130

Greater Birmingham Convention &
    Visitors' Center
Commerce Center
Birmingham, AL 35203

Alaska

Alaska Division of Tourism
Pouch E, State Capitol
Juneau, AK 99811

Anchorage Convention & Visitors'
    Bureau
201 E. Third Avenue
Anchorage, AK 99501

Arizona

Arizona Office of Tourism
3507 N. Central, Ste. 506
Phoenix, AZ 85012

Phoenix and Valley of the Sun
    Convention & Visitors' Bureau
505 N. 2nd St., Ste. 300
Phoenix, AZ 85004

Arkansas

Tourism Division
Arkansas Department of Parks &
    Tourism
One Capitol Mall
Little Rock, AR 72201

Greater Little Rock Chamber of
    Commerce
One Spring Street
Little Rock, AR 72203

California

California Division of Tourism
1400 Tenth Street
Sacramento, CA 95814

Los Angeles Convention & Visitors'
    Bureau
Attn: Visitor Inquiry Mail
P.O. Box 71608
505 S. Flower Street
Los Angeles, CA 90071

San Diego Convention & Visitors'
    Bureau
1200 Third Avenue, Ste. 824
San Diego, CA 92101

San Francisco Convention &
    Visitors' Bureau
P.O. Box 6977
San Francisco, CA 94101

Colorado

Colorado Tourism Board
1625 Broadway, Ste. 1700
Denver, CO 80202

Denver Convention & Visitors'
    Bureau
225 W. Colfax Avenue
Denver, CO 80202

Connecticut

State of Connecticut Tourism
    Division
Dept. of Economic Development
210 Washington Street
Hartford, CT 06106

Delaware

Delaware Tourism Office
99 Kings Highway
P.O. Box 1401
Dover, DE 19903

District of Columbia

Washington Convention & Visitors'
    Association
1575 Eye St., Ste. 250
Washington, DC 20005

Florida

Florida Tourism Office
Department of Commerce
107 W. Gaines St., Rm. 505
Tallahassee, FL 32304

Jacksonville Convention & Visitors'
 Bureau
206 Hogan Street
Jacksonville, FL 32202

Miami Metro-Dade Tourism Dept.
234 W. Flagler, 2nd Floor
Miami, FL 33130

St. Petersburg Chamber of
 Commerce
4th Street and 3rd Avenue S.
St. Petersburg, FL 33701

Georgia

Georgia Dept. of Industry & Trade
 Tourist Division
P.O. Box 1776
Atlanta, GA 30301

Atlanta Convention & Visitors'
 Bureau
Harris Tower, Ste. 200
233 Peachtree St. NE
Atlanta, GA 30043

Hawaii

Hawaii Visitors' Bureau
2270 Kalakaua Avenue
Honolulu, HI 96815

Idaho

Idaho Travel
State House, Room 108
Boise, ID 83720

Illinois

Chicago Convention & Tourism
 Bureau
McCormick Place on the Lake
Chicago, IL 60616

Springfield Convention & Visitors'
 Bureau
219 S. Fifth Street
Springfield, IL 62701

Indiana

Tourism Development Division
Indiana Department of Commerce
440 N. Meridian Street
Indianapolis, IN 46204

Indianapolis Convention & Visitors'
 Bureau
100 S. Capitol Avenue
Indianapolis, IN 46225

Iowa

Iowa Development Commission
 Tourism Group
600 E. Court Avenue
Des Moines, IA 50309

Des Moines Chamber of Commerce
800 High Street
Des Moines, IA 50307

Kansas

Kansas Travel & Tourism Division
Dept. of Commerce
400 W. 8th, 5th Floor
Topeka, KS 66603

Kentucky

Kentucky Department of Public
 Information
Division of Travel & Promotion
Capitol Annex
Frankfort, KY 40601

Louisville Convention & Visitors'
 Bureau
Founders Square
501 Muhammed Ali Blvd.
Louisville, KY 40202

100 NEW PLACES

Louisiana

Louisiana Office of Tourism
Inquiries Section
P.O. Box 44291
Baton Rouge, LA 70804

Greater New Orleans Tourism &
  Convention Commission
334 Royal Street
New Orleans, LA 70130

Maine

The Maine Publicity Bureau
97 Winthrop Street
Hollowell, ME 04347

Chamber of Commerce of Greater
  Portland
142 Free Street
Portland, ME 04101

Maryland

Maryland Office of Tourist
  Development
Department of Economic &
  Community Development
1748 Forest Drive
Annapolis, MD 21401

Baltimore Area Convention &
  Visitors' Bureau
102 St. Paul Street
Baltimore, MD 21202

Massachusetts

Massachusetts Visitors' Information
Prudential Center
P.O. Box 490
Boston, MA 02199

Greater Boston Chamber of
  Commerce
125 High Street
Boston, MA 02110

Michigan

Michigan Travel Bureau
P.O. Box 30226
Lansing, MI 48909

Metropolitan Detroit Convention &
  Visitors' Bureau
100 Renaissance Center
Ste. 1950
Detroit, MI 48243

Flint Convention & Visitors' Bureau
Northbank Center, Ste. 101-A
400 N. Saginaw
Flint, MI 48502

Minnesota

Dept. of Economic Development
Vacation Information Center
480 Cedar, Hanover Building
St. Paul, MN 55101

Greater Minneapolis Chamber of
  Commerce
15 S. Fifth Street
Minneapolis, MN 55402

St. Paul Chamber of Commerce
445 Minnesota Street
N. Central Tower, Ste. 701
St. Paul, MN 55104

Mississippi

Mississippi Division of Tourism
P.O. Box 22825
Jackson, MS 39205

Natchez-Adams County Chamber of
  Commerce
300 N. Commerce Street
Natchez, MS 39120

Missouri

Missouri Division of Tourism
P.O. Box 1055
Jefferson City, MO 65102

Convention & Visitors' Bureau of
  Greater Kansas City
City Center Square
1100 Main, Ste. 2550
Kansas City, MO 64105

101
NEW PLACES

Convention & Visitors' Bureau of
   Greater St. Louis
10 Broadway, 3rd Floor
St. Louis, MO 63103

Montana

Montana Department of Commerce
Travel Promotion
1424 9th Avenue
Helena, MT 59620

Nebraska

Nebraska Department of Economic
   Development
Travel & Tourism Division
301 Centennial Mall S.
P.O. Box 94666
Lincoln, NE 68509

Visitors' Council Greater Omaha
   Chamber of Commerce
1819 Farnam St., Ste. 1200
Omaha, NE 68183

Nevada

Nevada Department of Economic
   Development
Tourism Division
Capitol Plaza
1100 E. Williams St., Ste. 106
Carson City, NV 89710

Las Vegas Convention & Visitors'
   Authority
3150 Paradise Road
Las Vegas, NV 89109

New Hampshire

New Hampshire Office of Vacation
   Travel
Division of Economic Development
P.O. Box 856
Concord, NH 03301

Greater Manchester Chamber of
   Commerce
Attention: Inquiries
57 Market Street
Manchester, NH 03101

New Jersey

New Jersey Division of Tourism
P.O. Box CN 384
Trenton, NJ 08625

Atlantic City Convention & Visitors'
   Bureau
16 Central Pier
Atlantic City, NJ 08401

New Mexico

New Mexico Department of
   Development
Tourist Division
113 Washington Avenue
Santa Fe, NM 87503

New York

I Love NY
Division of Tourism
99 Washington Avenue
Albany, NY 12245

Buffalo Area Chamber of Commerce
Convention & Tourism Division
107 Delaware Avenue
Buffalo, NY 14202

New York Convention & Visitors'
   Bureau, Inc.
Two Columbus Circle
New York, NY 10019

North Carolina

North Carolina Department of
   Commerce
Travel & Tourism Division
430 N. Salisbury Street
Raleigh, NC 27611

Greater Charlotte Chamber of
Commerce
P.O. Box 32785
Charlotte, NC 28232

North Dakota

North Dakota Travel Department
Highway Department Building
State Capitol
Bismark, ND 58501

Ohio

Ohio Office of Travel & Tourism
P.O. Box 1001
30 E. Broad Street
Columbus, OH 43216

Cincinnati Convention & Visitors'
Bureau
200 W. Fifth Street
Cincinnati, OH 45202

Convention & Visitors' Bureau of
Greater Cleveland
1301 E. Sixth Street
Cleveland, OH 44114

Columbus Area Chamber of
Commerce
50 W. Broad Street
Columbus, OH 43216

Oklahoma

Literature Distribution Center
Oklahoma Tourism & Recreation
Department
215 28th Street NE
Oklahoma City, OK 73105

Oregon

Oregon Dept. of Transportation
Travel Information
State Transportation Building
Salem, OR 97310

Greater Portland Convention &
Visitors' Bureau
26 SW Salmon Street
Portland, OR 97204

Pennsylvania

Pennsylvania Dept. of Commerce
Bureau of Travel Development
416 Forum Building
Harrisburg, PA 17120

Philadelphia Convention & Visitors'
Bureau
1525 John F. Kennedy Blvd.
Philadelphia, PA 19102

Greater Pittsburgh Chamber of
Commerce
Chamber of Commerce Building
Pittsburgh, PA 15219

Rhode Island

Rhode Island Department of
Economic Development
Tourist Promotion Division
Seven Jackson Walkway
Providence, RI 02903

Convention & Visitors' Bureau
Newport County Chamber of
Commerce
P.O. Box 237
Newport, RI 02840

South Carolina

South Carolina Department of
Parks, Recreation, & Tourism
Division of Tourism
P.O. Box 71
Columbia, SC 29202

South Dakota

South Dakota Dept. of Economic &
Tourism Development
221 S. Central
Pierre, SD 57501

Tennessee

Tennessee Tourist Development
P.O. Box 23170
Nashville, TN 37203

NEW PLACES

Knoxvisit the Knoxville Area Council
    for Conventions & Visitors
P.O. Box 15012
Knoxville, TN 37901

Memphis Convention & Vistors'
    Bureau
12 S. Main, Ste. 107
Memphis, TN 38103

Nashville Chamber of Commerce
161 Fourth Avenue N.
Nashville, TN 37219

Texas

Texas Tourist Development Agency
P.O. Box 12008, Capitol Station
Austin, TX 78711

Dallas Convention & Vistors' Bureau
1507 Pacific Avenue
Dallas, TX 75201

Fort Worth Chamber of Commerce
700 Throckmorton Street
Fort Worth, TX 76102

Houston Chamber of Commerce
1006 Main Street
Houston, TX 77002

San Antonio Chamber of Commerce
602 Hemisfair Plaza Way
P.O. Box 2277
San Antonio, TX 78206

Utah

Utah Travel Council
Council Hall, Capitol Hill
Salt Lake City, UT 84114

Salt Lake Valley Convention &
    Vistors' Bureau
Salt Palace, Ste. 200
Salt Lake City, UT 84101

Vermont

Vermont Travel Division
Agency of Development &
    Community Affairs
61 Elm Street
Montpelier, VT 05602

Lake Champlain Regional Chamber
    of Commerce
P.O. Box 453
Burlington, VT 05402

Virginia

Virginia Division of Tourism
202 N. Ninth St., Ste. 500
Richmond, VA 23219

Norfolk Convention & Vistors'
    Bureau
Monticello Arcade
Norfolk, VA 23510

Washington

Department of Commerce &
    Economic Development
Tourism Development
101 General Administration Bldg.
Olympia, WA 98504

Seattle-King County Convention &
    Vistors' Bureau
1815 Seventh Avenue
Seattle, WA 98101

W. Virginia

W. Virginia Office of Economic &
    Community Development
Travel Development Division
1900 E. Washington
Building 6, Room B-564
Charleston, WV 25305

Wisconsin

Greater Milwaukee Convention &
    Visitors' Bureau, Inc.
756 N. Milwaukee Street
Milwaukee, WI 53202

Wyoming

Wyoming Travel Commission
I-25 and College Drive
Cheyenne, WY 82002

Casper Area Chamber of Commerce
P.O. Box 399
Casper, WY 82602

europe on a postcard

Travel to Europe on a postcard. With tourism packets from the European countries listed here, you can go on the sightseeing tour of your life!

directions: Use a postcard. (Free)

ask for: Tourism Information

write to: The tourism office nearest you for the countries that interest you most.

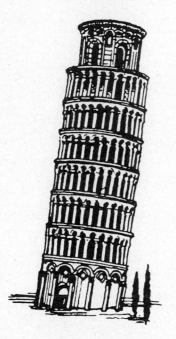

Belgium

Belgian National Tourist Office
745 Fifth Avenue., Ste. 714
New York, NY 10151

Denmark

Danish Tourist Board
655 Third Avenue
New York, NY 10017

Danish Tourist Board
150 N. Michigan Ave., Ste. 2110
Chicago, IL 60601

Danish Tourist Board
8929 Wilshire Blvd., Ste. 300
Beverly Hills, CA 90211

Finland

Finnish Tourist Board
655 Third Avenue
New York, NY 10017

France

French Government Tourist Office
610 Fifth Avenue, Room 222
New York, NY 10020

French Government Tourist Office
9401 Wilshire Blvd., Ste. 314
Los Angeles, CA 90112

French Government Tourist Office
645 N. Michigan Avenue, Ste. 630
Chicago, IL 60611

French Government Tourist Office
World Trade Center, Ste. 103
P.O. Box 58610
Dallas, TX 75258

Germany

German National Tourist Office
747 Third Avenue
New York, NY 10017

German National Tourist Office
444 S. Flower Street
Los Angeles, CA 90071

Great Britain (for teachers only)

British Tourist Authority
40 W. 57th Street
New York, NY 10019

Greece

Greek National Tourist Organization
645 Fifth Avenue
New York, NY 10022

Greek National Tourist Organization
168 N. Michigan Avenue
Chicago, IL 60601

Greek National Tourist Organization
31 State Street
Boston, MA 02109

Greek National Tourist Organization
611 W. 6th Street, Room 1998
Los Angeles, CA 90017

Iceland

Iceland Tourist Board
655 Third Avenue
New York, NY 10017

Ireland

Irish Tourist Board
590 Fifth Avenue
New York, NY 10036

Irish Tourist Board
230 N. Michigan Avenue
Chicago, IL 60601

Irish Tourist Board
1880 Century Park E.
Los Angeles, CA 90067

Irish Tourist Board
625 Market Street
San Francisco, CA 94105

Italy

Italian Government Travel Office
630 Fifth Avenue
New York, NY 10111

Italian Government Travel Office
500 N. Michigan Avenue
Chicago, IL 60611

Italian Government Travel Office
360 Post Street, Ste. 801
San Francisco, CA 94108

Luxembourg

Luxembourg National Tourist Office
801 Second Avenue
New York, NY 10017

Netherlands

Netherlands National Tourist Office
437 Madison Avenue
New York, NY 10022

Netherlands National Tourist Office
605 Market Street, Ste. 401
San Francisco, CA 94105

Norway

Norwegian Tourist Board
655 Third Avenue
New York, NY 10017

Portugal

Portuguese National Tourist Office
548 Fifth Avenue
New York, NY 10036

Spain

Spanish National Tourist Office
665 Fifth Avenue
New York, NY 10022

Spanish National Tourist Office
845 N. Michigan Avenue
Chicago, IL 60611

Spanish National Tourist Office
One Hallidie Plaza
San Francisco, CA 94102

Sweden

Swedish Tourist Board
655 Third Avenue
New York, NY 10017

Swedish Tourist Board
150 N. Michigan Ave., Ste. 2110
Chicago, IL 60601

Swedish Tourist Board
8929 Wilshire Blvd., Ste. 300
Beverly Hills, CA 90211

Yugoslavia

Yugoslav National Tourist Office
630 Fifth Avenue, Room 280
New York, NY 10111

terrific hieroglyphic!

Maybe the best thing in this six-page foldout about ancient and modern Egypt is the hieroglyphic chart. It shows and translates 24 signs from an alphabet that is thousands of years old. Or maybe the best thing is the information about pyramids, temples, and tombs.

directions: Use paper and an envelope. You must enclose a long, self-addressed, stamped envelope.

ask for: Egypt Tourism Folder

write to: Egyptian Tourist Authority
630 Fifth Avenue
New York, NY 10111

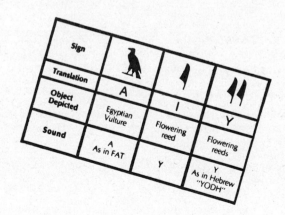

picture perfect

When you send for the Switzerland Children's Kit, you'll get a poster of the Swiss countryside that's so big and beautiful, you'll think you can walk right into the landscape.

directions: Use a postcard. (Free)

ask for: Children's Kit

write to: Swiss National Tourist Office
608 Fifth Avenue
New York, NY 10020

right next door

This packet about Austria, Switzerland's neighbor, is full of tourist information and features colorful pictures of the Austrian Alps.

directions: Use a postcard. (Free)

ask for: Tourist Information Packet

write to: Austrian National Tourist Office
500 Fifth Avenue
New York, NY 10110

index

Use this index to find the items and topics in which you're most interested. The book's contents are listed by subject area (like history, music, and people), by type of item (like maps and stickers), or both.

109
INDEX

**110
INDEX**

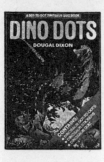

Dino Dots
by Dougal Dixon

This fascinating connect-the-dots puzzle book features 25 prehistoric wonders. Each page also presents a "name this dinosaur" quiz. Included are facts about each dinosaur.

Order #2250

Rub–a–Dub–Dub, Science in the Tub
by James Lewis

Now preschool kids can learn science while they splash and play in the tub. These thirty-three fun experiments, complete with step–by–step illustrations, introduce basic concepts like why some things sink and some things float, how sailboats sail, how to make and blow bubbles, how funnels work, how to make little waves (instead of big ones) and more.

Order #2270

Learn While You Scrub, Science in the Tub
by James Lewis

Now school-age kids can learn science while they splash and play in the tub. Here are forty-one fun experiments that introduce five- to nine-year-olds to concepts like how a pump works, why water evaporates, what causes a whirlpool, how air pressure works, how water changes an object's weight, why water magnifies objects, and more.

Order #2350

Measure, Pour and Mix, Kitchen Science Tricks
by James Lewis

Now kids can whip up simple scientific experiments right in the kitchen with a little help from Mom and Dad. Here are 32 fun experiments, complete with step by step instructions that show how to make frost using ice cubes and salt, how to make a xylophone with glasses of water, and more

Order #2370

Weird Wonders & Bizarre Blunders
by Brad Schreiber

Here's a book for people who enjoy Guinness' most amazing records and Ripley's most unbelievable facts, but wish they went one step further into the zany zone. It's the weirdest collection of world records, and the funniest.

Order #4120

Almost Grown-Up
by Claire Patterson
Illustrated by Lindsay Quilter

Here's a frank and funny guide that sensitively explains to kids what's happening to their bodies and feelings as they go through puberty. It's the least embarrassing book about the most embarrassing subject.

Order #2290

Professor Percival Pinkerton's Most Perplexing Puzzles
by Christopher Maslanka

This cleverly written and illustrated book of brainteasers boasts a wide variety of math, science, logic and verbal puzzles. It also includes helpful hints and solutions.

Order #6070

Order Form

Quantity	Title	Author	Order No.	Unit Cost	Total
	1,2,3...Play with me!	Paré, R.	2240	$12.95	
	A,B,C...Play with me!	Paré, R.	2230	$12.95	
	Almost Grown-Up	Patterson, C.	2290	$4.95	
	Dino Dots	Dixon, D.	2250	$4.95	
	Free Stuff for Kids, 14th Edition	FS Editors	2190	$4.95	
	How to Help Your Child Succeed in School	Stainback/Stainback	1320	$5.95	
	How to Survive High School	Lansky/Dorfman	4050	$5.95	
	It's My Party!	Croasdale/Davis	2390	$5.95	
	Learn While You Scrub, Science in the Tub	Lewis, J.	2350	$6.95	
	Measure, Pour and Mix, Kitchen Science Tricks	Lewis, J.	2370	$5.95	
	My First Years Photo Album		3139	$15.95	
	Prof. Pinkerton's Most Perplexing Puzzles	Maslanka, C.	6070	$4.95	
	Rub-a-Dub-Dub, Science in the Tub	Lewis, J.	2270	$5.95	
	Stork didn't bring me	Hébert, M.	2220	$12.95	
	Weird Wonders, Bizarre Blunders	Schreiber, B.	4120	$4.95	
	Wordplay	Thiesen/King	2200	$5.95	

Meadowbrook Press

Subtotal	
Shipping and Handling (see below)	
MN residents add 6% sales tax	
Total	

YES, please send me the books indicated above. Add $1.25 shipping and handling for the first book and $.50 for each additional book. Add $2.00 to total for books shipped to Canada. Overseas postage will be billed. Allow up to 4 weeks for delivery. Send check or money order payable to Meadowbrook Press. No cash or C.O.D.'s please. Quantity discounts available upon request. Prices subject to change without notice.

Send book(s) to:

Name _____

Address _____

City _____ State _____ Zip _____

☐ Check enclosed for $_____, payable to Meadowbrook Press

☐ Charge to my credit card (for purchases of $10.00 or more only)

☐ Phone Orders call: (800) 338-2232 (for purchases of $10.00 or more only)

Account # _____ ☐ Visa ☐ MasterCard

Signature _____ Expiration date _____

Meadowbrook Press, 18318 Minnetonka Boulevard, Deephaven, MN 55391
(612) 473-5400   Toll free (800) 338-2232